# That I May Know Him

## KAY ARTHUR
## DAVID LAWSON

HARVEST HOUSE™ PUBLISHERS

EUGENE, OREGON

*Cover by Koechel Peterson & Associates, Inc., Minneapolis, Minnesota.*

**The New Inductive Study Series**
THAT I MAY KNOW HIM

Copyright © 1998 by Precept Ministries International
Published by Harvest House Publishers
Eugene, Oregon 97402

Library of Congress Cataloging-in-Publication Data

Arthur, Kay, 1933–
    That I may know him  /  Kay Arthur and David Lawson.
        p. cm. — (The new inductive study series)
    ISBN 0-7369-0809-9
    1. Bible. N.T. Philippians—Study and teaching.    2. Bible. N.T. Colossians—Study and teaching.    I. Lawson, David.  II. Title.    III. Series: Arthur, Kay, 1933–
The new inductive study series.
    BS2705.5.A77    1998
    227'.6'0071—dc21                                                      98-36529
                                                                              CIP

**Printed in the United States of America.**

02  03  04  05  06  07  08  09  10  / BP /  10  9  8  7  6  5  4  3  2  1

# CONTENTS

∾∾∾∾∾

# *H*OW TO *G*ET *S*TARTED...

You are about to begin a study which will transform your approach, understanding, and comprehension of the Word of God.

As you work through this book, there are several things that will help you get the most from your study time.

## FIRST: Supplies for the Study

As you study the books of Philippians and Colossians you will need four things in addition to this book:

1. A Bible that you are willing to mark in. The marking is essential. An ideal Bible for this purpose is *The New Inductive Study Bible (NISB)*. The *NISB* is in a single-column text format with larger, easy-to-read type, which is ideal for marking. The margins around the text are wide for note-taking.

The *NISB* also has instructions for studying each book of the Bible, but it does not contain any commentary on the text, nor is it compiled from any theological stance. Its purpose is to teach you how to discern truth for yourself through the inductive method of study. (The various charts and maps that you will find in this study guide are taken from the *NISB*.)

Whatever Bible you use, just know you will need to mark in it, which brings me to the second item you will need...

2. A fine-point, four-color ballpoint pen or various colored fine-point pens that you can use to write in your Bible.

3. Colored pencils or an eight-color Pentel pencil (available at most office supply stores).

4. A composition book or notebook for working on your assignments and recording your insights.

## SECOND: Suggestions on How to Study

1. As you study Philippians and Colossians, you'll find specific instructions for each day's study. The study should take you between 15 and 25 minutes a day. However, if you find the lessons too long, simply do what you can. To do a little is better than doing nothing. Don't be an all-or-nothing person when it comes to Bible study.

2. As you read each chapter, train yourself to think through the text by asking the "5 Ws and an H": who, what, when, where, why, and how. Posing questions like these helps you see exactly what the Word of God is saying.

    a. **What** is the chapter about?

    b. **Who** are the main characters?

    c. **When** does this event or teaching take place?

    d. **Where** does this happen?

    e. **Why** is this being done or said?

    f. **How** did this happen?

3. Watch for and mark key words. A **key word** is an important word that is used repeatedly by the author in order to convey his message to the reader. This signals its importance. Some key words will show up throughout the entire book, while others will be concentrated in specific chapters or segments.

When you mark a key word, mark its synonyms (words that have the same meaning within a particular context) and any pronouns (such as *he, his, she, her, it, we, they, us, our, you, their, them*) in the same way you have marked the key word. We will give you various ideas and suggestions in your daily assignments for how you can mark different key words. These are only suggestions. Mark the words in the way that you choose.

---

NOTE: We have identified key words as they are translated in the New American Standard translation. If you are using the King James Version (KJV), the New King James Version (NKJV), or the New International Version (NIV) these words may be translated differently. If a footnote number appears by the key word, its equivalent is located on the footnote page in the back of the book.

Marking key words for easy identification can be done by using colors, symbols, or a combination of colors and symbols. For example, one of the key words in Philippians is *joy*. You could draw a box around ⬚ joy (like this) and color it orange. When you mark key words the same way throughout your Bible, it gives you an instant awareness of their presence throughout all of Scripture.

When you start marking key words, it is easy to forget how you are marking them. You may wish to use the bottom portion of the perforated card in the back of this book as a bookmark and write the key words on it.

4. Because geographic locations are important in the epistles (or letters), mark them as well. You might make a note on your key word bookmark to remember to mark locations. Maps are included in this study so you can look up the locations where Paul traveled. This will enable you to put his letters into context geographically.

5. Charts entitled PHILIPPIANS AT A GLANCE and COLOSSIANS AT A GLANCE are located at the end of each study. As you complete your study of each chapter of the Scripture, record the main theme of that chapter on the appropriate chart. A chapter theme is a brief description or summary of the main idea or event discussed. Recording the themes will help you remember the main focus of each chapter. It will also give you a complete "at a glance" synopsis of the book once you finish the study.

6. Each day, as you finish your lesson, take some time to think about what you read. Ask your heavenly Father how you can apply these insights to your own life. You may wish to journal these insights in your notebook as "Lessons for Life."

7. Most importantly, begin your study with prayer. Don't start without it. Ask God to allow the Holy Spirit to soften your heart so you can hear His voice and to show you the truths of His Word as you study.

## THIRD: The Structure of the Study

This study is designed so that there is an assignment for every day of the week. This gets you into the Word of God on a daily basis. You will notice the seventh day of each week has several different features:

Here you will find a verse or two from that week's study to memorize and thus *Store in Your Heart*. This will help you focus on a major truth covered in your study that week.

### Questions for Discussion or Individual Study

Seeking to answer these questions will help you reason through some key issues in the study. Make sure the answers you give are supported from the Bible itself. Before you decide what the passage of Scripture means, make sure you look at it in the light of its context. The context of a passage is simply the Scriptures which precede and follow the passage you are studying. If you come to a passage that is difficult to understand, reserve your interpretation for a time when you can study the full context of the passage in greater depth.

### Thought for the Week

This section is to help you apply what you've learned. Here, a little of our theology will inevitably come to the surface. We don't expect you to always agree with us. We trust you will think through what is said in light of the context of the Word of God and then determine what you will believe.

Are you ready?

It is time now to begin the study and join thousands who are awed at the way God has enriched their relationship with Him and deepened their understanding of His Word through studying the Scriptures. May God open the eyes of your understanding that you may behold wonderful things in His Word. Remember, to study or not to study is a matter of choice first, discipline second. It's a matter of the heart. On what or whom are you setting your heart?

Have fun as you study, for you are about to meet and be reminded of the One who loves you....

# PHILIPPIANS

# Knowing Him, Knowing Joy

❧❧❧❧

Life is tough. Sometimes it's filled with pain and betrayal—or if not betrayal, at least the tensions of interpersonal relationships that can divide us and separate us from what we need most—unconditional love and fellowship with others.

Sometimes our circumstances seem so difficult, so hard, and so confining that it seems we live in a prison with invisible bars and a door that has rusted shut.

Yet…despite it all, whatever may come your way, do you realize that you can have a deep and abiding joy? That's the message of the book of Philippians. During the six weeks of this study, you're going to discover for yourself how to have joy no matter what the circumstances of your life.

So whatever it may cost in the way of discipline to stay with this study, do it. I guarantee you that it will be worth the effort!

# OH TO BE ABLE TO SAY, "TO LIVE IS CHRIST" AND MEAN IT!

How important is it to you to share the gospel? Important enough that you would go to prison if necessary? Wouldn't it be wonderful if your heart was that set on Christ and on the defense of the gospel?

## DAY ONE

When you study a book of the Bible, you should first observe the text to see exactly what it says. Careful and thorough observation is the key to handling the Word of God accurately, as 2 Timothy 2:15 says. If you will learn to handle it carefully, you will not be ashamed when you see your Lord face-to-face. Remember it is God's Word, not man's, and it is to be respected accordingly.

Your assignment for today is to read through Philippians to gain a general overview of this letter's content.

Make a section in your notebook entitled OVERVIEW OF PHILIPPIANS. In this section, you will need several pages. You might title your comments in your notebook, MY FIRST IMPRESSIONS OF PHILIPPIANS. Then as you read, note who is writing this epistle and to whom.

When you finish, take a few minutes to record any general impressions you have about this book. By first impressions, we mean . . .

> what kind of a letter is it?

> what prompted the writing (the circumstances or occasion)?

> what is its tone; i.e., instructive, encouraging, admonishing, warning, correcting?

> what seems to be happening?

> what is the purpose of the letter?

Many times the purpose is not obvious on the first reading, but it will be when you dig deeper into the text.

## DAY TWO

When you observe a book of the Bible, you should begin by looking for the obvious. Usually the most obvious thing is the people who are mentioned. Therefore, today you are to read the first chapter of Philippians and color or underline every reference to the author in a specific color—for example, color or underline each reference blue. This includes any personal pronouns such as *I, my, me,* or *we.*

When you finish, look at each reference you marked. Then, in your notebook, begin a list of what you learn about the author(s) of this epistle. Title it FACTS ABOUT THE AUTHOR.

At this point, don't record all the details of what he is telling the Philippians to do because we will look at this later. Simply record any facts that would tell you something about Paul as a person. For example, note who he is, where he is, why he is there, what is transpiring, or what has happened before. Doing this will help you discover the historical context of this epistle: when it was written and what was occurring at this time.

Also watch for anything that would give you a clue as to why he is writing this letter. For instance, would verse 9 or verse 27 indicate some concern he feels? If so, make a column in your notebook called POSSIBLE REASONS FOR WRITING. Then list any insights you observe in this column. (You'll pick up more possibilities as you mark the references to the Philippians in the remaining weeks of study.)

As you list your observations, note the chapter and verse from which you gleaned your information. When you finish, think about what you can learn from the author's example and what you can learn for your own life.

## DAY THREE

Read Philippians 2 again, color-coding each reference to the author. Record your observations in your notebook as you did yesterday.

## DAY FOUR

Read Philippians 3 and once again mark every reference to Paul. However, do not take time today to make a list of what you learn about Paul because it would be very detailed and take too long. We will save this exercise for the fourth week of our study of Philippians when it will mean more because of the content of the chapter. Leave room in your notebook to add these insights later.

## DAY FIVE

You guessed it! Once again mark every reference to Paul as you read chapter 4. List what you learn about Paul in 4:21,22. When you finish your assignment, review the list of all you have recorded about the author of Philippians.

Now what do you learn from your list about Paul? Look at it carefully and see if it tells you who Paul is, where he is, why he is there, who is with him, what his circumstances are, and why he is writing. These are all important for your study of Philippians.

What you are doing by reviewing your observations on Paul is asking the investigative questions of who, what, when, where, why, and how. We call these the 5 Ws and an H.

Considering all that you have observed from the overall context of Philippians, what do you think is the main theme of this letter? In other words, what is it about? What phrases and ideas are repeated? What is Paul's desire for the Philippians? Record the main theme on the PHILIPPIANS AT A GLANCE chart on page 45.

Record your insights in the overview section of your notebook.

## DAY SIX

Today we want to get a brief historical understanding of Paul's relationship to the Philippians. Read Acts 15:36–17:1,

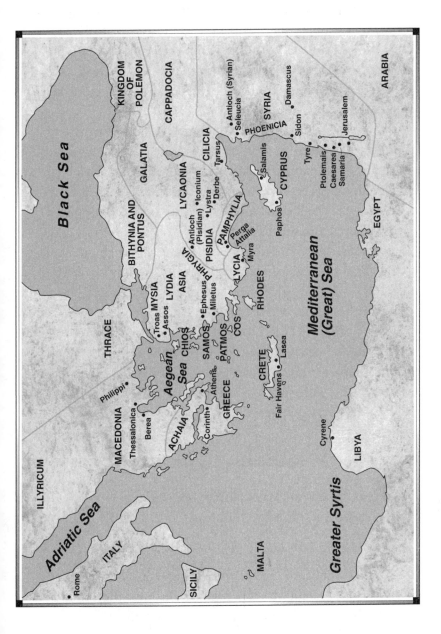

which will tell you of Paul's first visit to Philippi during his second missionary journey (recorded in Acts 15:36–18:22).

Look at the map of the regions Paul would eventually visit on his three missionary journeys. As you read Acts 15:36–17:1, trace the route he took on this second journey that led him to Philippi.

After his third missionary journey, Paul returned to Jerusalem, where he was arrested. After spending three years in Caesarea as a prisoner of the Roman Empire, Paul called upon his rights as a Roman citizen and, appealing to Caesar, was transferred to Rome. Read Acts 28:16-30 and note where Paul is when the book of Acts comes to an end. How does this compare to what you learned about Paul from reading Philippians this week? (Carefully note Acts 28:16.)

You will find a chart, SEQUENCE OF EVENTS IN PAUL'S LIFE AFTER HIS CONVERSION, on page 17. Examine the chart, noting the years of Paul's first Roman imprisonment and the dates when Philippians was written. Record this information on the PHILIPPIANS AT A GLANCE chart on page 45.

## DAY SEVEN

Store in your heart: Philippians 1:21.
Read and discuss: Philippians 1:12-26; 4:13-23.

*QUESTIONS FOR DISCUSSION OR INDIVIDUAL STUDY*

∾ What were some of the first impressions you recorded in your notebook after reading through the book of Philippians?

# Sequence of Events in Paul's Life After His Conversion*

*There are differing opinions on these dates.
For continuity's sake this chart will be the basis for all dates pertaining to Paul's life.*

| Scripture | Year A.D. | Event |
|---|---|---|
| Acts 9:1-25 | 33–34 | Conversion, time in Damascus |
| | 35–47 | Mostly silent years, except we know that Paul: |
| Galatians 1:17 | | 1. Spent time in Arabia and Damascus |
| Acts 9:26; Galatians 1:18 | | 2. Made first visit to Jerusalem — 3 years |
| Acts 9:30–11:26 Galatians 1:21 | | 3. Went to Tarsus, Syria-Cilicia area |
| Acts 11:26 | | 4. Was with Barnabas in Antioch |
| Acts 11:29,30 | | 5. With Barnabas took relief to brethren in Judea — Paul's second visit to Jerusalem |
| Acts 12:23 | 44 | Herod Agrippa I dies |
| Acts 12:25 | | 6. Returned to Antioch; was sent out with Barnabas by church at Antioch |
| Acts 13:4–14:26 | 47–48 | **First missionary journey:** *Galatians written* |
| | | Proconsul Sergius Paulus on Paphos is datable |
| Acts 15:1-35; Galatians 2:1 | 49 | Apostolic Council at Jerusalem—Paul visits Jerusalem (compare Acts 15 with Galatians 2:1) |
| Acts 15:36–18:22 | 49–51 | **Second missionary journey:** *1 and 2 Thessalonians written;* 1½ years in Corinth, Acts 18:11 |
| | 51–52 | Gallio known to be proconsul in Corinth |
| Acts 18:23–21:17 | 52–56 | **Third missionary journey:** *1 and 2 Corinthians and Romans written* |
| Acts 21:18–23:35 | 56 | Paul goes to Jerusalem and is arrested; held in Caesarea |
| Acts 24–26 | 57–59 | Appearance before Felix and Drusilla; before Festus —appeals to Caesar; before Agrippa—datable |
| Acts 27–28:15 | 59–60 | Paul goes from Caesarea to Rome |
| Acts 28:16-31 | 60–62 | First Roman imprisonment: *Ephesians, Philemon, Colossians,* and *Philippians* written— 2 years in prison |
| | 62 | Paul's release; possible trip to Spain |
| | 62 | Paul in Macedonia: *1 Timothy written* |
| | 62 | Paul goes to Crete: *Titus written* |
| | 63–64 | Paul taken to Rome and imprisoned: *2 Timothy written* |
| | 64 | Paul is absent from the body and present with the Lord |

The bracket spanning the rows from 35–47 through 47–48 is labeled "14 years" and "Galatians 2:1".

*(Others put Paul's conversion about A.D. 35, his death at A.D. 68.)*

ᘉ What did you learn about the apostle Paul from marking the various references to him in this epistle? If you are using this book for a group study and you have a white board or static images sheets, list the class observations for the whole group to see. (Remember, all your insights should come from the book of Philippians, so the class should be prepared to back up its insights with Scripture.)

ᘉ What did you learn about Paul's first visit to the city of Philippi? Where is this city located—what country is it in?

ᘉ How was the church first established in Philippi?

a. What were the events surrounding it?
b. Where did Paul find his first converts?
c. How long was Paul in Philippi?
d. Why did he leave there?

ᘉ Where was Paul when he wrote the epistle to the Philippians?

a. What was Paul's purpose in writing the letter to the Philippians?
b. Discuss the verses that give you these insights.

ᘉ What did you learn about Paul this week that you would like to see mirrored in your own life?

## THOUGHT FOR THE WEEK

Wouldn't it be wonderful to live in such a way that, with confidence, you could say the very words recorded for eternity by the apostle Paul, "For to me, to live is Christ and to die is gain" (Philippians 1:21)? Wouldn't it be wonderful to know that your life had been spent for the defense of the gospel?

We know from 1 Corinthians 9:24-27 and 2 Corinthians 5:10 that Paul was acutely aware of his accountability to the Lord. Paul had been appointed by God to proclaim the gospel to Jew and Gentile. He knew he was a steward of the mysteries of God, and he ordered his life accordingly. The Lord Jesus Christ and His glorious gospel were the focus of Paul's life, and he made every moment and every situation count. Thus, we have to assume that if God had taken Paul home to heaven during the time of his first Roman imprisonment, he would not have been ashamed.

If Paul's passion, as stated in Philippians 1:20, becomes our passion, then we will have the same confidence. Think about these words, Beloved. Meditate on them during the week. Use them as a divine plumb line against all that you do…and watch how it affects your decisions, your responses, and your relationships with others and with God.

"According to my earnest expectation and hope, that I shall not be put to shame in anything, but that with all boldness, Christ will even now, as always, be exalted in my body, whether by life or by death" (Philippians 1:20).

# Is Joy Possible
# Even When I Feel Imprisoned
# by My Circumstances?

Does it bother you when people put you down because of your faith—when they ridicule you, talk about you behind your back, ignore or pass over you when it comes to recognition in the workplace and the community? Does it hurt, make you angry, or make you wonder what you are doing wrong? Does the pain and persecution tempt you not to be as open about your faith? Hold on...persevere...stand firm. There is an answer for your dilemma as we will discover this week.

## DAY ONE

Read through Philippians 1 again. Mark in a second distinctive color every reference to the Philippians. Make sure you mark the pronouns and synonyms such as *saints* or *brethren*.[1] Then, when you finish, make another section in your notebook entitled FACTS ABOUT THE PHILIPPIANS and record what you observe about them from this chapter.

## DAY TWO

When we began our study, I pointed out that references to people are the easiest thing to see when we observe the text of a book of the Bible. As you read through the first chapter, who (other than Paul) is mentioned more often than anyone else? When you discover this, mark every reference to Him in another distinctive color or symbol.

## DAY THREE

A reading of the book of Philippians will show that the Lord Jesus Christ is front and center stage in this brief, joyous epistle.

There are several key words used throughout the letter to the Philippians that you will want to mark as you observe its content. If you have not read the "How to Get Started" section in the front of this book, it would be beneficial to do so before you go any further. It will explain the value of marking your key words—*joy*[2] *(rejoice), mind(s)*[3] *(attitude*[4]*),* and *gospel.* Another word that would be good to mark in this first chapter is *imprisonment.*[5] Choose a distinctive way or color for marking each of these words. Then list and color code them on a 3 x 5 card or on the perforated card in the back of this book. Once you finish your bookmark, read Philippians 1 and mark every occurrence of any of these words.

## DAY FOUR

Whenever I read my Bible, I like to mark any reference to *pray(er)* or *supplication*[6] in its own distinguishing way, for I want to learn what the Bible itself has to say in regard to prayer. As with all doctrines, men and women sometimes teach some fanciful ideas on the subject of prayer that can be contrary to the Scriptures or not present in the Word of God. Therefore, it is good to build your theology on any given subject by what the Word of God teaches throughout its pages.

Today, let's discover what insights Philippians 1 gives us on the subject of prayer. Choose a way you would like to mark all references to *prayer* throughout your Bible, and then mark all the references in Philippians 1 accordingly.

*(By the way, you might want to reserve a portion of one of the blank pages in the front or back of your Bible for the recording of key words that you would like to mark in a consistent manner as you read through the Word of God. This would be a good place not only to record the word, but to mark it so that you will always have it there as a reminder of how you have chosen to mark each particular word.)*

When you finish, record in your notebook what you learn about prayer from this chapter. Then, as you bring your study to a close, use Paul's prayer in Philippians 1:9-11 to pray for those God lays upon your heart.

## DAY FIVE

Read Philippians 1:12-26. What do you learn about Paul's circumstances from this passage? What is taking place? Record your insights in your notebook. As you do, watch for Paul's response. Note how he is handling his situation and why. What—who—is Paul's passion?

In your notebook, list what you learn about Jesus Christ from marking the references to Him in 1:1-26. Then read 1 Corinthians 15:1-11. Keep in mind that 1 Corinthians was also written by Paul.

From this passage, what would you say are the main points of the gospel which we learned in Philippians that Paul is determined to defend? List these points in your notebook.

## DAY SIX

In 1:27-30, Paul gives instructions to the church at Philippi. Record what you learn from this passage. What are they to do? Why?

In your notebook, list what you observe in chapter 1 from marking *gospel* and *joy (rejoice)*. What do you learn about each of these? How does it minister to you personally?

Having spent a week observing Philippians 1, what would you say is the main subject or teaching of this chapter? Record your answer on the PHILIPPIANS AT A GLANCE chart on page 45. Record it on the line for chapter 1.

## DAY SEVEN

Store in your heart: Philippians 1:29.
Read and discuss: Philippians 1; 1 Corinthians 15:1-11.

### QUESTIONS FOR DISCUSSION OR INDIVIDUAL STUDY

∾ What did you learn from marking the word *gospel* in Philippians 1? Who is central to the gospel? What is the gospel of Jesus Christ all about? If you are going to share the gospel, what is the essence of its message as stated in 1 Corinthians 15:1-11? *Grace of God*

∞ According to Philippians 1:27-30, what was Paul's concern in respect to the gospel? What do you learn in chapter 1 about the reception of the gospel in Philippi? *Phili. Conduct*

∞ From Philippians 1:27-30, what do you see that accompanies salvation in Jesus Christ? Have you experienced this as a Christian? How did you handle it? In this particular passage, what is Paul's admonition to the church? *People will oppose me / To suffer for Christ*

∞ From reading Philippians 1, what do you learn about Paul and what it cost him to defend the gospel of Jesus Christ? *Prisonment*

∞ What did you learn in the first chapter of Philippians that would help Paul to stand firm as he suffered for the gospel? What did Paul request of the Philippians? *Prayers of the Church, Holy Spirit*

∞ What did you learn about prayer? What is the hardest aspect of prayer for you?

∞ You marked the key words *joy* (*rejoice*) this week. What do you learn about them from this chapter?

∞ As you studied Philippians 1, what had the biggest impact upon you?

## THOUGHT FOR THE WEEK

As we clearly saw in this week's study, suffering is a gift from our Lord—a gift that accompanies salvation; therefore, it is something we are to expect. We must remember, Beloved, that we are living in the last days, which began with the coming of our Lord to earth. Since we are in the final hour, can we really expect to avoid suffering as God's kingdom clashes with the kingdom of darkness? The kingdom of darkness and its ruler of old, the serpent who is the devil—Satan—goes about as a roaring lion, seeking whom he may devour.

However, though the lion roars, we need not fear. The Lion of the tribe of Judah, as the Lamb of God, overcame him when He paid in full the penalty for our sin.

According to Hebrews 2, when Jesus Christ became your Savior and all your sins were no longer imputed to your account, the devil, who previously had the power of death because of our sin, was defeated. Sin gave Satan his power; the blood of Christ took it away.

Death's "stinger" has been removed. Jesus holds the keys of death and hell. Therefore, remember that although it is given to you to suffer for Christ's sake, you are to stand firm. You are not alone because Jesus is at the door. He will soon come to take you home. He who began a good work in you, the work of salvation, will perfect it until the day of Christ Jesus. Suffering is part of His perfecting work, Beloved, so live in such a way as to be sincere and blameless until the day of Christ, filled with the fruit of righteousness which comes through Jesus Christ.

# TAKING CARE OF THAT ATTITUDE!

Attitudes—we all have them. But it's the bad ones that are hard to handle, isn't it? Whether it's ours or someone else's, what do we do in response to a rude, self-absorbed attitude?

## DAY ONE

As you begin your study, ask God to help you understand how He wants you to interact with others.

Read through Philippians 2. As you read, mark the key words on your bookmark.

If you will take the time to read Philippians 2 aloud, it will help you memorize the content of this chapter. When you file it in your memory, it'll be an easy recall when you need it.

## DAY TWO

Read Philippians 2 again and mark every reference to *Jesus Christ* or *Lord*. He's your key resource for maintaining a good attitude. Watch for and mark in the same way all the pronouns (*He, Himself, Him, who* [if they refer to Christ]).

Then mark any reference to the *Holy Spirit* in another distinctive way. It would be good to mark the Holy Spirit in the same way throughout your Bible. Doing this and taking careful note of what you learn will help you recognize erroneous teachings about the Holy Spirit.

## DAY THREE

Read Philippians 2 aloud and mark every reference to the Philippians.

## DAY FOUR

Read Philippians 2 again carefully, noting every place you marked a reference to the Philippians. Using the list you began in chapter 1, record what you learn about them from chapter 2. As you read through the chapter, look for any instructions Paul gives to them that you might have missed earlier, since in some verses the "you" referring to the Philippians is assumed or understood. For example, in verse 2 it says, "make my joy complete"— the direct address "you" is missing, but it is assumed. Therefore, this is an instruction you might miss if you simply look for each place Paul directly addresses the Philippians by name. Don't forget to write down the "address" (chapter and verse) in which you find your information. Then put a star by every instruction given to the Philippian church.

When you finish, think about your own life. Do you see anything in these instructions that applies to you because you are a child of God?

## DAY FIVE

You guessed it; read Philippians 2 again! (You're really going to know this book, aren't you?)

Notice that Paul mentions two other men in this chapter: Timothy and Epaphroditus. Mark each of these men in a distinctive way and list in your notebook what you learn about each of them.

Who did they model? Can you learn anything from them? What kind of attitude did these men have?

## DAY SIX

Look at each reference to the Lord Jesus Christ that you marked earlier in Philippians 2 and list in your notebook what you learn about Him. Then think about what you've just learned about Jesus Christ. This is truth, Beloved—truth that will never change, never alter. You can stake your life on it!

Did you notice the phrase "the day of Christ" in verse 16? It is also used in Philippians 1:6,10. Mark these three references in a distinctive way. You might want to put a cloud around them, like this: **the day of Christ** and then color them in a special color.

The day of Christ could be the time when Jesus returns for His own, takes them to heaven, and then has them stand before Him at an event called "the judgment seat of Christ." If you would like to examine the Scriptures which refer to this time, you'll find them in 1 Thessalonians 4:13-18; 1 Corinthians 15:51-54; 2 Corinthians 5:10; and Romans 14:10-12.

Record the main theme or subject that is covered in chapter 2 on the PHILIPPIANS AT A GLANCE chart on page 45.

## DAY SEVEN

Store in your heart: Philippians 2:5-8, or if that is too much, memorize Philippians 2:3,4.
Read and discuss: Philippians 2:1-17.

*QUESTIONS FOR DISCUSSION OR INDIVIDUAL STUDY*

ю One of the key words on your bookmark that you marked this week was *mind* or *attitude*. What did you learn from marking these words? What did Paul want the Philippians to do? *Being like minded having the same zone. our attitude should be the same as christ.*

ю According to Philippians 2:1, what has every child of God found in or received by belonging to the Lord Jesus Christ? How does Philippians 2:2 relate to 2:1? What point is Paul trying to make? *encouragement in christ*

ю What was the mind of Christ—the attitude of Christ—like? According to Philippians 2:5-8, how did this attitude manifest itself? What did God do in return? *became in human likeness*

ю How would a person demonstrate this kind of attitude, the attitude of Christ, in his or her daily life? How would verses 3 and 4 help you answer this question? *look out for the interest of others*

ю Have you ever found yourself in situations where you had the opportunity to demonstrate Jesus' attitude and failed to? Is it your habit to take what Philippians 2:1 says you have "in Christ" and share it with others? Have you learned anything that could help you?

∽ Did Timothy and/or Epaphroditus manifest the mind or attitude of Christ in any way? How do you know? Do you see Paul demonstrate this attitude in this chapter? If so, where?

∽ How do you think Philippians 2:12-16 connects with what Paul has said in chapter 2 up to this point? How do you measure up or should you?

∽ In 2:17, how do you think Paul is being poured out as a drink offering? Stop and think about what you have learned regarding his circumstances. Why is he where he is?

∽ Has God spoken to you this week? How? What do you think could come about in your life as a result of what you've learned?

## THOUGHT FOR THE WEEK

When God tells us, through Paul, to "work out" our own salvation with fear and trembling, the phrase *work out* means "to carry out to completion." God is telling us that we are to allow Him to carry out the work He is doing in us. We are not to quench or grieve the Spirit of God.

The key to pleasing God, to having the mind of Christ, is to lay down our lives for Him, to release our supposed rights or privileges, to surrender them, and to let God have His full way in us. As a believer, you share all that is God's in common with the Holy Spirit—this is the fellowship of the Holy Spirit. You have found encouragement in Christ, and have received the consolation of His love. As Romans 5 tells us, God has shed His love abroad in our hearts through the Holy Spirit who has been given to us. You have found affection because you are beloved of God. You have received compassion because you have become God's child.

Since all of this is yours, Beloved, and since God has worked it in you, let it flow out to others. Let it flow to other believers and to the world. Be of the same mind, maintain the same love, remain united in spirit, be intent on one purpose: glorifying God by walking worthy of the gospel of our Lord Jesus Christ. Live above reproach. Show the world what Jesus Christ is like. Let Christ's attitude be in you. When you do this, you'll see that others notice! The world is longing for such an example. Give it to them, Beloved.

# TORN BETWEEN HOLDING ON TO EVERYTHING OR GIVING IT ALL UP FOR JESUS

What is most precious to you, of the utmost importance? What are your goals, your passions, your ambitions? What have you counted on for your identity?

Would you be willing to let go of it for the sake of Jesus Christ and His kingdom?

## DAY ONE

Philippians 3 is another awesome chapter! Read it aloud, and mark the key words on your bookmark. As you do, think about what you learn from each occurrence of these key words.

Also mark every reference to *Jesus Christ* and to the *Spirit of God* (which is the Holy Spirit).

## DAY TWO

Read Philippians 3 again, marking every reference to the Philippians. In this chapter, who is the real focus—the Philippians or Paul? If you see any new insights on the Philippians, add them to your list.

## DAY THREE

Today list in your notebook everything you learn about Paul from this chapter. Do this by reading Philippians 3 again. As you read, make sure you didn't miss any reference to Paul when you read the chapter during your first week's study.

In verses 10 and 11 there is a simple list of what Paul wanted. You can mark simple lists right in the text by putting a number above each of the things in the list. For instance, you can mark the text like this example: If you want to lose weight, when you go to the store [1]park as far as possible from the entrance to the store, [2]don't shop when you are hungry, [3]only buy the items on your list, etc.

When you finish your list on Paul, take a good look at all you have learned about Paul's heart for God and for His Son, our Lord Jesus Christ. How does this hit you?

## DAY FOUR

When you made your list about Paul, did you notice another key word that is repeated in this chapter—*things*? Read Philippians 3 again and mark the word *thing(s)*[7] and any pronoun used for *things*.

Unless you want to, it is not necessary to make a list about Jesus Christ since you learned so much when you made your list about Paul. Simply note on your list what you learn about Jesus from 3:20,21.

Now think about the things that are important to you. You might want to list them in your notebook. When you finish, take a prayerful look at them. Ask God if any of these "things" get in the way of being what God would have you be, or living the way God would have you live.

## DAY FIVE

In Philippians 3:9 Paul said that he wanted a righteousness which comes from God on the basis of faith. Faith is also mentioned in the first three chapters of Philippians. Read through these chapters and mark every reference to *faith*. Since faith comes by hearing and hearing by the Word of Christ—God—you might want to mark faith like this: **faith** and color it green. It will remind you where faith comes from.

When you finish, list everything you learn from marking the word *faith*. Then think about what Paul means by the "righteousness…which is through faith in Christ" and "on the basis of faith." You might also want to mark the word *resurrection* and its pronouns. Then in your notebook, list what you learn from marking *resurrection*.

## DAY SIX

In Philippians 3:17-19, Paul warns the Philippians about others—those he refers to as "many." Write in your notebook what Paul warns the Philippians about in 3:2,18,19. Note how they are described. (If you want added understanding on false circumcision, read Romans 2:28,29.)

Now, looking at the text, note in verse 17 who they have as an example for how they are to walk.

If you have time, look up the following Scriptures and write down in your notebook what you observe in these verses and how they parallel with Philippians 3:17:

1. 1 Corinthians 4:16
2. 1 Corinthians 11:1
3. 1 Thessalonians 1:6,7 (Paul wrote 1 Thessalonians.)

That's quite an amazing thing to say to someone, isn't it? Could you say the same thing to another person—"Be an imitator of me, even as I am of Jesus Christ"? Take a moment to evaluate what another Christian could imitate in your life. Could you tell someone to follow your example, even as you follow Christ's?

Close out today's study time by recording the main subject of Philippians 3 on the PHILIPPIANS AT A GLANCE chart.

## DAY SEVEN

Store in your heart: Philippians 3:7,8 or Philippians 3:14.

Read and discuss: Philippians 3.

*QUESTIONS FOR DISCUSSION OR INDIVIDUAL STUDY*

∾ What is Paul's major concern in Philippians 3? How does this connect with its being a safeguard to remind them to rejoice in the Lord? What could the people rejoice in—boast in, take pride in? What is Paul's warning near the end of chapter 3?

∾ There is a true circumcision and a false one. In Jeremiah 4:4, as God reproves His people for their sin, He says, "Circumcise yourselves to the LORD and remove the foreskins of your heart. . . ." They were circumcised physically, but not spiritually. From observing Philippians 3, what would you conclude about the difference between true and false circumcision?

∞ What do you think Paul meant when he said he put no confidence in the flesh? According to Philippians 3:4-6, what did Paul have going for him, according to the flesh? What could Paul boast about or glory in if he wanted to?

∞ Why could Paul tell them to imitate him, to follow his example? What was Paul's example?

∞ How important was it to Paul to know Christ? In this passage, do you think Paul is talking about salvation or about knowing Christ more fully—as much as He can be known? What are your reasons for your answer?

∞ Paul said he wanted to "attain to the resurrection from the dead" (3:11). If the "resurrection from the dead" means becoming all you can be in Christ because you died with Him and were raised with Him to walk in newness of life (as Romans 6 says), what do you think Paul means in this verse?

∞ What did Paul have to do to attain to the resurrection from the dead, to reach the goal for the prize of the upward call of God in Christ Jesus?

∞ To reach that same goal, what must you do? What verses in Philippians 3 give you instruction on this?

∞ What will it cost you personally to reach this goal? Are you willing to pay the price? Is it worth the cost? Think about or discuss how God spoke to you personally this week from Philippians 3.

## THOUGHT FOR THE WEEK

O Beloved, do you eagerly await our Savior, the Lord Jesus Christ, who will transform this body of ours into conformity with the body of His glory? His coming becomes very precious to us when the passion of our life is Christ.

It was for the righteousness which came through faith that Paul counted all things as loss—considered them but dung. He put no confidence in his flesh. Whatever was gain to him, he counted as loss. His passion was to be identified with Christ—to know Him and the power of His resurrection and the fellowship of His sufferings...to be conformed to Christ's death. The cross of Christ was not Paul's enemy, but his friend.

Paul realized that he had not yet attained, but he still didn't look back. Instead, he forgot those things which were behind, and reached forward to press on toward the goal of the prize of the upward call in Christ Jesus.

Here, Beloved, is our example. Surely if we follow Paul as our example we will be able to say, "I have fought the good fight, I have finished the course, I have kept the faith; in the future there is laid up for me the crown of righteousness ..." (2 Timothy 4:7,8). Paul attained the righteousness he so desired! And so can you, Beloved, if you will count all things as loss, even as Paul did. Press on, Valiant One. Press on.

# WHERE DOES A PERSON FIND PEACE AND CONTENTMENT?

Do you ever find that your peace or security is tied up in the circumstances of your life? Do you live in an intermittent state of anxiety? Do you ever wonder if a time of peace and plenty will come? Or, if not plenty, at least peace! Or can there be peace without having plenty? Let's see what Philippians 4 has to say.

## DAY ONE

Read through this wonderfully practical fourth chapter of Philippians. Mark every reference to the Philippians and add to your list any new insights you learn.

## DAY TWO

As you read Philippians 4 aloud, mark the key words which appear in this chapter. Also mark every reference to the *Lord Jesus Christ* and to *prayer (supplication)* as you marked them in chapter 1.

## DAY THREE

Now look at how Philippians 4 begins. What is the "therefore" there for? *Therefore* is a term of conclusion. Look through the preceding verses and summarize the message Paul sets before them in verse 1.

This is not the first time Paul has exhorted them to stand firm or hold fast. Look up the following verses in Philippians and list in your notebook under OVERVIEW OF PHILIPPIANS what you learn from these verses in the framework of their context: Philippians 1:27; 2:16; and 4:1.

Read Philippians 4:1-9 and list Paul's instructions to the Philippians. Be as detailed as possible, for you will find many practical guidelines for your own life in these instructions. Record your insights on these paragraphs in your notebook under the title PAUL'S INSTRUCTIONS TO THE PHILIPPIANS IN CHAPTER 4.

Note how 4:9 corresponds with what Paul said in Philippians 3:17.

## DAY FOUR

Read Philippians 4:10-12. Mark the word *circumstance(s)*[8] in a distinctive way. Then record everything you learn about circumstances on the list you're keeping on the Philippians.

## DAY FIVE

Today read Philippians 4 and add any new insights on Paul to your list. When you finish, review all you've recorded. You have quite a profile on Paul just from this short epistle.

Also list everything you learn about Jesus Christ from this chapter. Then review your list about the Lord. Put a star by the things which mean the most to you right now. Then take a few minutes to thank God for Jesus: for who He is, all He has done, and what He will do for you.

## DAY SIX

Are you, or is someone you know and love, in difficult circumstances? What can you learn and share with them from Philippians 4:10-19? Make a list and record it in your notebook.

Throughout this book you have marked the following words and their synonyms: *joy,*[9] *mind (attitude),*[10] and *gospel.* You began a list in your notebook in Week Two, Day Six for the words *joy* and *gospel.* Add to these lists now any other insights you've gleaned from this chapter. Also compile a list of all you've observed about *mind* or *attitude.* These lists will give you an overview of this epistle's teaching on these three things. You can record your list under chapter 4 or in the overview section.

Finally, record the main theme or subject of Philippians 4 on the PHILIPPIANS AT A GLANCE chart at the end of this chapter. Fill in all the blank spaces that you can on this chart. When you finish, take a good look at it. You have a wonderful synopsis of the book of Philippians—a task you completed on your own by carefully observing the text.

While there is much more that you could study at a greater depth in this book, you are to be commended, dear student, because you have laid a solid foundation by careful observation. You have also become familiar with the general content of this "epistle of joy."

If you have a *New Inductive Study Bible,* you will want to transfer all these observations to your Bible. You will also want to write the main theme of each chapter at the beginning of the text of each chapter in the place designated in your *NISB.*

## DAY SEVEN

Store in your heart: Philippians 4:6,7 or Philippians 4:11,13.

Read and discuss: Philippians 4.

### QUESTIONS FOR DISCUSSION OR INDIVIDUAL STUDY

∾ What is the main teaching of Philippians 4?

∾ As Paul brings his short letter (epistle) to a close, what did you learn about joy and rejoicing throughout the book of Philippians? Review the list you made. What are Paul's final words on the subject in chapter 4? What is his example? What have you learned that you can apply to your own life?

∾ What did you learn this week about anxiety? How are you to handle it? What will happen if you do?

∾ What have you learned from this chapter about your thought life? What is your mind to dwell on? How do you think you can do that?

∾ What did you learn about the various circumstances in which Paul had been? What did he learn from them? How did he handle the adverse or difficult circumstances? Again, what did you learn for your own life? Is it easier said than done? Can it be done? How do you know?

∞ What do you learn about giving from this chapter? Be as specific as possible, considering each point in Philippians 4:14-19. What is the context of the promise in Philippians 4:19? How can you apply this to your life?

∞ You marked the word *mind* or *attitude* throughout the book of Philippians. What did you learn from marking this word throughout the book? Summarize your insights. How can this information help you in a practical way?

∞ You also marked the word *gospel.* Review what you learned from marking it throughout the book. To what does the gospel call us? Where does its proclamation lead? Is it always easy? What are we to do?

∞ Finally, what spoke to you most powerfully in your study of Philippians? What hit home the hardest? What has stayed with you throughout the study? What is the easiest or hardest thing for you to believe or do? What are you going to do?

## THOUGHT FOR THE WEEK

Peace. Peace and plenty. We all want it, but can we have it? Peace? Yes. Plenty? No! Philippians 4 makes it clear that in spite of life's difficulties we can rejoice. In fact, we are told to rejoice, for the rejoicing is not in our circumstances, but in the Lord who is in control of every circumstance of life.

How well Paul demonstrates this in his epistle to the Philippians, a letter which was preserved in the pages of

God's Book, written for our doctrine, reproof, correction, and instruction in righteousness. The Bible is a book that helps us know how to handle every situation of life. As we see in Philippians 4, whether anxiety or great need, God's presence and His promises are there, sufficient for all we really need. We can do—we can bear—all things through our precious Lord Jesus Christ who strengthens us.

Now, may we take the things which we have learned, received, heard, and seen in Paul and practice them. If we do, we can rest assured that the God of peace will be with us.

# PHILIPPIANS AT A GLANCE

**Theme of Philippians:** Give up everything and Live and Die For Jesus Christ.

SEGMENT
DIVISIONS

| COMMAND TO: | JESUS IS: | PAUL'S EXAMPLE: | CHAPTER THEMES |
|---|---|---|---|
| Refeal the Gospel | 1:21 MY LIFE | To Die Preaching Christ | 1 Year A.D 60·62 1st Roman Imprisonment |
| | | | 2 |
| 3:17 FOLLOW PAUL'S EXAMPLE | | | 3 Be imistaters of Christ. |
| | | 4:11 LEARNED TO BE CONTENT IN HIS CIRCUMSTANCES | 4 |

*Author:*
Paul

*Historical Setting:*

*Purpose:*

*Key Words:*

# COLOSSIANS

# KNOWING HIM, KNOWING HIS POWER

Paul sat under house arrest in Rome. The accommodations were not bad, but his freedom was gone! A visitor came—a man who had come to believe in Jesus Christ after hearing Paul preach the truth of a risen Savior. "Good to see you again. Of course I remember you. From Ephesus, right? How is your walk with the Lord, brother?" the conversation might have gone. "You started a church in Colossae? Wonderful! Trouble? What kind of trouble?"

After Epaphras explained the trouble that was destroying his congregation, Paul called his scribe and began to dictate a letter. A short letter to a small insignificant market town. But it was a powerful letter with the imprint of God upon it. What could we, almost 2000 years later, learn from such a letter? The Truth.

# THAT *I* MAY BE FILLED
# WITH A *K*NOWLEDGE OF *H*IS *W*ILL

## DAY ONE

As you begin a study of any book of the Bible, careful observation of the text is the key to accurate interpretation. Today your assignment is to read through the book of Colossians in one sitting. As you read, note who the letter is from and to whom it is written.

When you finish, make a section in your notebook entitled OVERVIEW OF COLOSSIANS. Take a few minutes and record any general impressions you have of this letter. Be sure to record who the author is and to whom the letter was written. If you have not read the "How to Get Started" section, take the time now to read it. It explains why you need the notebook.

## DAY TWO

In Bible study you always want to look first for the obvious. People, places, and events are the easiest things to see. Read Colossians 1:1–2:5 and chapter 4. Mark every reference to the author(s), including pronouns that refer to him, such as *I, my, me,* or *we.* Mark them in a specific color, such as blue. When you finish, begin a list in your notebook about the author. As you write your insights, note the chapter and verse. You'll want to leave room to add to this list throughout this study.

## DAY THREE

Today read Colossians 1:1–2:5 again and mark every reference to the recipients (i.e., *you*). Again, you will want to use a specific color such as red. In your notebook, list what you learn about the recipients (just as you did yesterday with Paul). Noting information about the author and recipients will help you better understand the purpose of the letter. You will add to this list throughout this study.

## DAY FOUR

Today your assignment is to read 1:1–2:5 again. This time mark every reference to *gospel*. Mark not only the word *gospel* but also any synonyms or pronouns Paul uses to refer to the gospel. Examples would be *word of truth*[1] or *it* in verses 5-7. At this point, start a bookmark for Colossians by listing on it key words and the symbols or colors you are using to identify them. As we suggested in the "How to Get Started" section, a 3 x 5 card or the bottom portion of the perforated card in the back will do. In your notebook, make a list of what you learn about the *gospel* after noting this word on your bookmark.

## DAY FIVE

Did you notice who founded the church at Colossae? Paul had never been to Colossae, but he had been to

Ephesus. It was probably there, under Paul's preaching, that Epaphras had been converted.

Today let's focus on Colossians 1:3-14. First, read the text and mark every reference to *God the Father* (including pronouns), and list in your notebook what you learn about God. I use a triangle for marking God the Father and a cross for marking the Son. Then read through this passage again watching for and marking the words *knowledge*[2] *(wisdom)*[3] and *pray (prayer, praying)*. Mark them in a distinctive way and add them to your bookmark.

## DAY SIX

Read through Colossians 1:3-14 again. Did you notice what Paul is praying and why he is praying it? List in your notebook what you learn about his prayer and the results that came from what he prayed. Are you being filled with a knowledge of His will? Are you walking in a manner worthy of the Lord? Take some time today to offer this prayer to the Father for yourself and also on behalf of someone else.

## DAY SEVEN

Store in your heart: Colossians 1:9,10.
Read and discuss: Colossians 1.

### QUESTIONS FOR DISCUSSION OR INDIVIDUAL STUDY

ॐ What did you learn as you read Colossians?

ॐ Who wrote this letter to the Colossians? Paul, Timothy, or both? How does the use of pronouns in Colossians 1:23-29 confirm this? What was Paul's relationship with the church at Colossae? Had he ever been there?

∿ Who brought the gospel to the Colossians? How had the gospel been effective in his life?

∿ What did you learn about the gospel from marking the references to it?

∿ Was the gospel effective in the lives of the believers in Colossae? How? Is the gospel having the same effect in your life that it had in the life of the Colossians? Should it?

∿ What did you learn about God this week? According to Colossians 1:13,14, what has God done for us? What is the connection between what you learned about God and the gospel?

∿ You marked the words *pray, prayer,* and *praying.* Discuss what you learned about the way Paul is praying in Colossians 1:3-14. What is Paul's reason for praying for them? What are the results of being "filled with the knowledge of His will in all spiritual wisdom and understanding"? Are you? Do your actions show it?

∿ How did the Holy Spirit minister to you this week as you learned about the gospel and prayer? What is one action that you will do differently because of what you have learned?

## THOUGHT FOR THE WEEK

As believers we have been delivered from the domain of darkness to the kingdom of light. The word "delivered" in Greek* has the idea of drawing something to yourself or

---

* From time to time we will look at the definition of a word in Greek. Since the New Testament was originally written in Koine Greek, sometimes it is helpful to go back to the Greek language to see the original meaning of a word. There are many study tools to help you if you would like to do this type of digging. One excellent book to help you understand how to do more in-depth study is *How to Study Your Bible* by Kay Arthur (Eugene, Oregon: Harvest House Publishers, 1994).

rescuing something. While we were under the power and authority of darkness, lost and unable to tell the truth from a lie, God rescued us; He drew us to Himself! What do we have in the new kingdom of light? We have "redemption, the forgiveness of sins" in Jesus Christ. The Greek word for *redemption* is also expressed by our English word "emancipation." We have been set free from slavery to sin; our debt has been paid. In Ephesians 1:7, we see that the price of our freedom was the blood of the Lamb.

Information like this is too important to keep secret, so Epaphras went home to Colossae to tell everyone he could the good news, the "gospel."

As you do this study, our prayer for you is that you will "be filled with the knowledge of His will in all spiritual wisdom and understanding, so that you may walk in a manner worthy of the Lord" in order to please Him, be strengthened, and increase in the knowledge of God. You are already on your way because you are in His Word. It is here that you will find the knowledge of His will and gain spiritual wisdom and understanding. So make it your goal, my friend, to walk in a manner worthy of the gospel.

# THAT I MAY KNOW THE TRUTH

If you're ready to see truth for yourself, if you're ready to see who Jesus Christ is, this is your week.

## DAY ONE

Did you notice whether or not Paul gives a reason for writing to those in Colossae? Sometimes the author states the purpose very plainly. Read Colossians 1:1–2:5 and look for Paul's reason for writing to the Colossians. You can find his purpose by seeing his concern for them. What danger, so to speak, were they in? Determine the danger to the Colossians that has caused Paul to pen this letter. Record your insights on the author's purpose for writing on the COLOSSIANS AT A GLANCE chart next to the author's purpose on page 97.

## DAY TWO

In Colossians 2:4, Paul indicates his concern for the Colossians, that someone might delude them with persuasive argument. The word *delude* means "to cheat by false reckoning." It carries the idea of an accountant using two sets of figures. A "persuasive argument" in the ancient Greek culture was used of a false but beautifully worded argument. Paul is worried that someone with a "silver tongue" and a "quick wit" will injure the church by manipulating the truth to reach a false conclusion, in other words, causing them to believe a lie.

Who does Paul discuss most in the verses we have been studying? Read Colossians 1 and mark every reference to *Jesus Christ.* Include in your marking every pronoun or synonym that refers to Christ such as *Lord, He,* or *Him.* Sometimes it is difficult to tell if the text is referring to God the Father or God the Son. Don't worry; if it were vital for us to know, the Holy Spirit would have made it plain. Do the best you can. Missing one pronoun won't affect your relationship with God one way or the other. Do not record what you learn about Jesus in your notebook; we will do that tomorrow.

By the way, *read,* do not scan. Bible study is a wonderful dining experience to be savored, not fast food.

## DAY *T*HREE

Today read chapter 1, noting every place you marked a reference to *Jesus Christ.* Record in your notebook what you learn about Him. Always try to keep a running list of what you learn about Christ.

What is Paul's focus with respect to Christ in chapter 1? Look at your list and determine the focus by asking who, what, when, where, why, and how about Christ.

## DAY FOUR

The list you made yesterday on Jesus Christ should have been an exciting one. Nowhere else in Scripture do we see so much about our Lord in so few verses. Let's read chapter 1 again; this time focusing on verses 9-29. Look for the word *all*[4] and mark it in a distinctive way. Read through this passage a second time and mark the words *knowledge (wisdom)* as you did last week (see page 51: end of first paragraph). Be sure to add both of these words to your bookmark. List in your notebook what this little three-letter word *all* helps you see about our Lord.

## DAY FIVE

Read Colossians 1:9-23 out loud. This helps you to remember what you have read. In verse 15, Paul begins the heart of his discussion of who Jesus Christ is.

Sometimes looking at other passages of Scripture or "cross-referencing" will help give a clearer understanding of what we are studying. Today let's read John 1:1-5 and 14-18. Start a new list in your notebook dealing with what you learn about Jesus from this cross-reference. (NOTE: Many of these cross-references are already printed in your Bible. They may be in a column or somewhere in the margin. They will be marked in the verse by a small letter in front of a word or phrase. Many of these references can be helpful, so you may want to record them in the margin of your Bible close to the appropriate text. Cross-referencing is very helpful when you do not have your study notes with you, because the cross-references are right in your Bible!) Starting a new list will help you to keep what you see about

Jesus in Colossians separate from what you see in other passages.

## DAY SIX

Sometimes difficult terms are explained in the text, but we can miss the explanation unless we read the text carefully and thoughtfully. Read Colossians 1:15-23 aloud and look for every reference to *first-born*. What does this term mean? Does the text explain it? Terms such as "for" and "so that" are conjunctions used to connect and explain thoughts. As you reason through this passage, watch how Paul uses these conjunctions in verses 16 and 18. What does this tell you about Jesus Christ? Understanding this will help insulate you against false belief systems.

## DAY SEVEN

Store in your heart: Colossians 1:15,16.

Read and Discuss: Colossians 1; Isaiah 11:1,2; John 1:1-18.

### QUESTIONS FOR DISCUSSION OR INDIVIDUAL STUDY

ॐ What is the concern that prompted Paul to pen this letter?

ॐ How does he address his concern? In other words, who does Paul talk about the most in these passages? Why?

ॐ What did you learn about Jesus Christ this week?

ॐ How did the word *all* help define who Jesus Christ is?

∾ What did you learn about *knowledge* (*wisdom*) this week? Read Isaiah 11:1,2 and compare it with what you learned about wisdom and knowledge from Colossians.

∾ Read John 1:1-18. Who is Jesus? Compare this with what you learned in Colossians 1.

∾ What does the phrase *first-born* mean? Does it mean Jesus is the first thing God created? Explain your answer from Scripture.

∾ Did the Holy Spirit encourage your heart in any way as you observed who Christ is and what He has done for you as a child of God?

## THOUGHT FOR THE WEEK

Paul's primary warning to the church at Colossae is found in Colossians 2:4, "I say this in order that no one may delude you with persuasive argument." Someone, perhaps a false teacher, was trying to convince the Colossians to believe a lie about Jesus Christ. The basic lie of all false religious systems has been to deny the deity of Christ or His sufficiency to save us. Many times this lie is made even more dangerous by the fact that the false teachers are within the church.

Are we immune to this problem in our culture, or do we also need to heed Paul's warning in 2:4? Are there people in churches today whose teachings about Jesus Christ do not line up with what you have seen in His Word this week? Your only protection against believing a lie and being deluded by a persuasive argument is to know the Truth. Who does Paul talk about most in this chapter? Who is the Way, the Truth, the Life?

The best way to address error is with a clear, positive statement of the truth. Paul begins in 1:15 to present a clear teaching on Jesus Christ which will combat the lies of the false teachers. The first thing that he says is Christ "is the image of the invisible God." The Greek word for "image" is *eikon.* It was used in classical Greek literature to describe the sun reflecting in a pool of water. In other words, Christ mirrors God for us. In Greek thought, the image shares reality with what it represents.* Christ is the Son of God. He is God incarnate.

Jesus is also called "the first-born of all creation." Some want this phrase to mean that Jesus is the first thing God created, His first Son. This passage cannot be interpreted that way. The Jews called God "the first-born of all creation" to signify His having created all things. Paul, being Jewish, is simply using a Jewish phrase to make his point that Jesus is God. In ancient cultures, the idea of "first-born" really implied rank and responsibility more than chronological birth order. In Exodus 4:22 and Jeremiah 31:9, Israel is called God's first-born. Was Israel the first group of people or the first nation on planet Earth? No, there are many nations centuries older. But Israel held the place of priority in God's plan. Did you notice the word *for* at the beginning of verse 16? Here Paul defines his use of "first-born" for those who are not familiar with Jewish thought.

Who is Jesus? In relation to God, He is His image. In relation to creation, He is the first-born...the One who is before all things. What does that mean to you?

---

* Cleon L. Rogers, Jr., Cleon L. Rogers III, *The New Linguistic and Exegetical Key to the Greek New Testament,* (Grand Rapids, MI: Zondervan Publishing House, 1998), p. 461.

# THAT *I* MAY *B*E RECONCILED TO *H*IM

What is the truth about your role in salvation? How much did you do for God? How much did He do for you? Are you ready to see the truth for yourself?

## DAY ONE

As a review, read Colossians 1:9-23. Read verses 15-20 again, but this time note Paul's use of the phrase *all things*. You have already marked *all* in your list of facts concerning Christ, but perhaps you didn't notice this phrase. What is Paul telling you about Christ? What is Christ's relationship to creation? Look at the world around you. Who created it for you to inhabit? Have you thanked God recently for His awesome creation?

## DAY TWO

Today read Colossians 1:9-28. Are you reading aloud? If not, try it. Compare what you have already seen about Christ from Colossians to what you can learn from Ephesians 1:18-23. Is Christ eternal? List in your notebook what you learn about Christ from this cross-reference.

## DAY THREE

Repetition is important to the learning process. Read Colossians 1:9-23 again. Compare what you learn about Christ in verse 18 with Ephesians 5:23. Who is the Head of the Church? The head is the one in authority. As members of the body, the Church, we are to be under the authority of Christ. What does this truth imply to you? Meditate on it and take it back to the Father in prayer, proclaiming your allegiance to the Head of the Church.

## DAY FOUR

Your assignment today is to read Colossians 1:19-23. In verses 15-18 Paul seems to show Christ's preeminence over all creation. In verses 19-23 there is a shift in focus. What is the subject Paul deals with in these verses? In Week One, you marked the word *you* when marking the recipients of this letter. What do you learn about the recipients and yourself in this passage?

## DAY FIVE

Once again, your assignment is to read Colossians 1:9-23. (I know you almost have this passage memorized, right? Great, keep on. Repetition increases retention.) List in your notebook what you learn from this passage about salvation. Read Romans 6:23 to see the penalty for our hostility toward God. Then read Romans 5:9,10 and learn what you can about our reconciliation and how it happened.

Spend some time in prayer today thanking God for the salvation He has offered all who will believe.

## DAY SIX

Today we want to identify the theme of chapter 1 and write it on your COLOSSIANS AT A GLANCE chart located on page 97. To do this, look for the main idea of the chapter. Who or what is Paul talking about most? Looking at the key words you have marked in the text, what is the heart of Paul's message in chapter 1? Sum up that message in a short phrase and enter it on your chart in the space for this chapter. Sometimes people hesitate in doing this part of the study for fear of getting the wrong answer. God is not going to be angry with what you write. He is excited that you are studying, and He loves you very much. Go ahead, think, pray, and put down what you have seen.

## DAY SEVEN

Store in your heart: Colossians 1:28.
Read and discuss: Colossians 1; Ephesians 1:18-22.

*QUESTIONS FOR DISCUSSION OR INDIVIDUAL STUDY*

∿ As you marked the phrase *all things* this week, what did the Lord show you? What is the relationship between "all things" and Christ?

∿ What did you learn about Christ's role in creation? According to Colossians 1:16, what has Christ created? How does this fact impact your day-to-day living?

∾ After Christ created everything, did He then abandon His creation to do the best it could, or is He still actively involved? Support your answer from the passages you studied this week.

∾ Who is the Head of the Church? In the human body, what does the head do? What about in the Church body?

∾ What new information did you learn about Christ from Ephesians 1:18-22?

∾ If Christ is the Creator, Sustainer, and the Head of the Church, what difference does any of this make in your life? In other words, what is your response to this truth?

∾ What did you learn about salvation this week? How were you described before you became a Christian? Have you ever seen yourself in this description? What has God done for you?

## THOUGHT FOR THE WEEK

Have you ever thought of yourself as a friend of God? God reconciled all things to Himself through the blood of the cross of Christ. *To reconcile* means to "exchange hostility for friendship." Because Jesus shed His blood to pay the penalty for our hostility, God has exchanged hostility for friendship. Are you a friend of God? Have you laid down your weapons and sworn allegiance to the King? To swear allegiance to the King is to place yourself under His authority, to allow Him to be the decision-maker in your life. This is an essential but sometimes overlooked issue in salvation. To continue to walk in hostility toward God (sin) and claim to be His friend is absurd. The purpose of the reconciliation is that we might be presented before Him holy and blameless and beyond reproach.

What part did we play in becoming a friend of God? What did we do to show God we were good enough? Carefully look at your list on salvation and you will see that it was all initiated by God. God qualified us to share in the inheritance of the saints in light. He delivered us from the domain of darkness. He transferred us into the kingdom of His Son. He gave us redemption, the forgiveness of sins in His Son. It was God who reconciled us.

Having said all of that, let me ask you, my friend, are you reconciled? It is not an issue of church attendance or membership. There are many members of local churches who are "hostile in mind" and "alienated" from Christ. Are you reconciled to God? Do you have a personal relationship with Jesus Christ? Have you ever asked God to forgive you for your hostility toward Him? He will forgive and reconcile you to Himself, and you will become like Him as He shows you how much He loves you.

# THAT I MAY KNOW ALL HE HAS DONE FOR ME

Do you realize that in the past three weeks you've learned more about Jesus than most people ever thought possible? And it's been without the help of a commentary. You have done it by being in His Word and seeing what it says. This week we're going to learn about God's greatest mystery.

## DAY ONE

Today we want to look at verses 24-29 of chapter 1. Start by reading these verses and marking every reference to the word *mystery*. When you finish, read Colossians 2:1-3 and 4:1-4. In your notebook begin a list of what you learn about the mystery. Now look at Ephesians 1:9,10 and 3:3-10, and add to your list any further information about the mystery. In the Bible a mystery is a truth that is hidden until it is revealed by God. What is God revealing to the Colossians and to you?

## DAY TWO

Are you excited? You have learned a lot about Jesus Christ, and there is still so much more to see. The exciting part is that you are seeing truth for yourself, straight from God's Word.

Read chapter 2 and mark every reference to *Christ,* just as you did in chapter 1. When you finish, list in your notebook what you learn. This is not a speed-reading contest, so slow down and enjoy the text.

## DAY THREE

The emphasis in chapter 1 is on who Christ is and what He has done. Paul's purpose is to combat the heresy (wrong teaching) false teachers were using to convince people to believe a lie (2:4). Instead of focusing on the lie, Paul defines the truth concerning Christ.

Some of the words you looked for in chapter 1 were *knowledge* and *wisdom.* Today, look at these same words in chapter 2. Check your bookmark to see how you marked them before and mark them in the same way. Read chapter 2 looking for each reference to these words. List in your notebook what you learn about wisdom and knowledge. In whom do you find true wisdom and knowledge? What gives the appearance of wisdom in self-made religion?

## DAY FOUR

Today let's consider two other important words in Colossians 2. We have already seen and marked *all* in chapter 1. While "all" tells us a lot about our Savior Jesus Christ, it also points us to some very important truths about ourselves. Read chapter 2 and mark every use of *all.* You will notice that every use of *all,* except one, has already been noted on your list about Christ. Take a moment to meditate on the truths you have seen. The second word you need to mark is *faith.* Add *faith* to your bookmark and then read chapter 2 and mark it in a distinctive way.

## DAY FIVE

Read Colossians 2 again, looking for every reference you marked for Jesus Christ. Generally, what is Paul teaching us about Christ in chapter 2? Your list from chapter 1 could be summed up as WHO CHRIST IS AND WHAT HE HAS DONE FOR YOU. What heading would you put in your notebook for the information you have about Christ from chapter 2?

Your list on Christ is getting significant, isn't it? If you have time, read through your list aloud, prayerfully thanking God for each thing you've learned about our awesome Savior.

## DAY SIX

Today let's focus on Colossians 1:24–2:4. You have already determined Paul's purpose for writing this letter. In the bigger picture, the solution to the danger of believing a lie is what Paul is teaching us about Christ. There is an exciting nugget of truth in verses 2 and 3.

Paul struggles for the church at Colossae. Why? What does he want for them? Read these verses carefully and list Paul's desire for them. It is God's desire for you also. Draw near to Christ.

## DAY SEVEN

Store in your heart: Colossians 1:26,27.

Read and discuss: Colossians 2; Isaiah 11:1-5; and 2 Peter 1:3,4.

## Questions for Discussion or Individual Study

ॐ Why did Paul feel the need to write this letter to the church at Colossae? What was he worried about?

ॐ Can you think of any examples of "persuasive arguments" that we might face today?

ॐ According to what you have studied this week, what is your protection against the danger of a "persuasive argument"?

ॐ In whom do you find wisdom and knowledge?

ॐ Discuss what you have learned this week about Jesus Christ.

ॐ How did the words *knowledge, wisdom,* and *all* help deepen your understanding of Christ?

ॐ What did you learn about the mystery? Who is the mystery? What is the mystery?

ॐ Discuss how you've summed up what Paul is telling you about Christ.

## Thought for the Week

The mystery of God is Christ in you, the hope of glory. As you did your study this week, did you realize that the Spirit of Christ lives in you? Old Testament saints did not understand this mystery. In 1 Peter 1:10-12, we see that the prophets of old made careful inquiry, trying to understand what the Spirit of Christ within them was indicating. The mystery that they struggled with has been revealed to you. The Holy Spirit of God came to dwell in you at the moment of salvation. You can walk in obedience to the truth because the Spirit of Truth lives in you! Christ in you, the hope of glory!

Why does Paul choose to discuss this mystery in this letter to the Colossians? There were false teachers denying the deity of our Lord, reducing Him to a lesser god. Paul confronts the error by a clear presentation of the truth, by presenting Jesus.

The only protection you have against believing a lie is knowing the truth. As you continue to study and to meditate on the Word of God, you are protecting yourself against error. You are in the Word now; keep on.

# THAT I MAY KNOW ALL HE HAS PROVIDED FOR ME

Don't you want to know everything God has for you? Don't you want to be all He has called you to be? If you do, then you must know the truth for yourself. This week we will learn more about what we have in Him.

## DAY ONE

Today read Colossians 2 and mark each time the recipients are mentioned. You read and marked the first five verses of chapter 2 during our first week of study together. Even though you have marked the information in these verses, read them again. Use the same symbol and color you did when you marked the recipients in chapter 1. When you finish, list in your notebook what you learn about the Colossians from this chapter.

## DAY TWO

Paul gives his first instruction to the Colossians in 2:6. Read 2:6,7 and note the instruction. You will want to start a list in your notebook entitled INSTRUCTIONS TO THE COLOSSIANS.

The false teachers were changing what the believers had been taught about Christ. How does this instruction to the believers relate to the problem? What had the believers received concerning Christ? What were they to continue to walk in, to believe about Christ?

You will also want to note in your notebook the four terms Paul uses to describe our walk in the Lord.

## DAY THREE

We have seen Paul's concern for the Colossians in 2:4. They were in danger of being deceived. In chapter 2, there are four additional warnings that address the danger they faced of being deluded by "persuasive arguments." A warning often sounds like an instruction, but it carries a sense of urgency—it reflects an immediate problem. Warnings have application today when we are faced with the same situations. Instructions in Paul's letters are more general, such as, "Children be obedient to your parents in all things." This is a very important instruction, but it doesn't carry the urgency of the warning in 2:4.

Read chapter 2 and mark the other warnings. One is indirect and phrased in question form, so read carefully. You may want to use a red "W" in the margin of your Bible to mark them. Then list the warnings in your notebook.

## DAY FOUR

Today read Colossians 2:8-15 to put yourself in context. We will focus on the second warning, which is in verse 8. After you have read this paragraph, read verse 8 again. In Greek, the phrase "empty deception" describes the philosophy which might take us captive. List in your notebook the three characteristics of this philosophy or system. (In other words, it is according to what two things and not according to what one thing?)

## DAY FIVE

This is getting exciting, isn't it? From your observation of Colossians 2:8, why are we to see to it that no one takes us captive? Read Colossians 2:9-15 and reason through the answer to this question. Remember, the word "for" in verse 9 is a conjunction and is used to connect and explain thoughts.

## DAY SIX

You have already noted what you learned about the recipients and what you've learned about Jesus Christ. Today may seem repetitive, but stay with it. It will be a blessing.

Read Colossians 2:8-15. Watch for *in Him* and *with Him*. Look at the list on Christ that you compiled last week from this chapter. It would be good to list what you have learned in the order in which it appears in these verses. Add what you learn about salvation to the list in your notebook that you began in Week Three. When you finish, take some time to meditate on this grace you have received.

## DAY SEVEN

Store in your heart: Colossians 2:9,10.
Read and discuss: Colossians 1:9–2:23.

## QUESTIONS FOR DISCUSSION OR INDIVIDUAL STUDY

∽ As you studied about the recipients of this letter, what did you learn about your salvation?

∽ What is the first instruction Paul gives the Colossians? How does this relate to what you discovered about salvation?

∽ What had the recipients received concerning Christ that they should "walk in"? Did they have a solid doctrine of Christ that could be their protection against unsound doctrine? What is it? Where have you seen that doctrine in this letter?

∽ What did you see this week that might take them captive? How is it described? Could this happen to us, or are we past such a danger?

∽ What is it that will protect you from being taken captive? In other words, according to Colossians 2:8-15 what do you have in Christ?

∽ What did you see this week that you had never seen before? In other words, what new truth did the Holy Spirit teach you this week?

### THOUGHT FOR THE WEEK

Colossians says that in Jesus Christ you have been made complete. Have you ever let that soak in? Have you let that roll over your mind like a soothing balm? Does life look daunting? Relax. In Him you have been made complete. Has God given you a task you are sure you are not up to? Rest easy. In Him you have been made complete.

Whatever situation arises, you have whatever spiritual resources you need, through the indwelling Holy Spirit.

The word translated "complete" in verse 10 is the verb form of the noun translated "fulness" in verse 9. Since Christ is fully God and fully man, and since we are in Christ, we are made full. In other words, we share in the fulness of Christ. Let that roll over your mind like a cool wave of living water.

# THAT I MAY KNOW HIS FREEDOM

It was for freedom that Christ set you free. What is this freedom? How do you walk in it? That will be our focus this week.

## DAY ONE

Today read Colossians 2:16-19. As we said earlier, when you see a "therefore" in Scripture, you want to always see what it is *there for*. We see in verse 16 that the "therefore" refers back to the preceding paragraph. Why are we not to allow someone to act as our judge in regard to food or drink? This is the same concept that is expressed in verse 8 of chapter 2. The danger is that someone would act as their judge concerning matters of philosophy, traditions of men, or the elementary principles of this world. Read Galatians 3:1-14. Will you walk by faith in freedom or by...?

## DAY TWO

Remember, the purpose of Paul's letter is to prevent them from believing a lie—you also saw this in Colossians 2:4. To insulate them against this danger, Paul tells them about Jesus—a lot about Jesus. He gives them four more warnings in addition to the primary one in 2:4. We have already looked at 2:8: "See to it that no one takes you captive through philosophy and empty deception."

Now that you have seen the flow of thought, we will look at the warnings a little more closely.

Today, read verses 16-23 of chapter 2, and then list the five things regarding which we are not to let someone act as our judge. When you have finished, read Hebrews 5:5-13 and 10:1. Compare these verses with what you have already learned.

## DAY THREE

Read Colossians 2:16-23 again. Someone wants to defraud you of your prize! List in your notebook the description of this person from verses 18 and 19. Does this match some people you know or hear about today? Are they taking stands on visions they have seen, instead of on the Word of God?

## DAY FOUR

Today let's read Colossians 2:16-23 again. In verse 19 we see that those who would defraud us do not hold fast to the Head. Look again at Colossians 1:18 to see who the Head is and who the body is. Also cross-reference Ephesians 1:22,23. Whose authority are these people ignoring?

## DAY FIVE

Today read Colossians 2:20–3:5. *Wisdom* is a word you have already marked. According to this passage, what has the appearance of wisdom? There is a simple list in verses

20-23. Write it in your notebook. Ask God if any of this applies directly to you. Record your theme for chapter 2 on the COLOSSIANS AT A GLANCE chart at the end of this section.

## DAY SIX

Read Colossians 2:20-23. Does this in any way sound like your experience as a Christian? Do you find yourself trying to live by the rules and regulations of a self-made religion, and still battling with the flesh? Do you fight against the desire to do what you know you should not do? It is an awful struggle. I know; I've been there. But there is good news—wonderful news: You don't have to live in defeat.

Read Colossians 3:1-4 and then read Galatians 5:1-6. What is the answer to legalism and all self-made religion?

## DAY SEVEN

Store in your heart: Colossians 3:1,2.
Read and discuss: Colossians 2; Galatians 5:1-6.

*QUESTIONS FOR DISCUSSION OR INDIVIDUAL STUDY*

∾ "Therefore" is a term of conclusion. As you read Colossians 2:16, what is the "therefore" *there for?* To what conclusion is Paul bringing his readers?

∾ Is someone acting as your judge in some area that is not vital to Christianity? If so, what area?

∾ Why is it wrong to be under such restrictions? How does Paul indicate our freedom from these rules?

∾ What are the characteristics of the enemy who would keep us in bondage to rules and regulations?

∾ What did you learn about the Head and the body this week?

∾ Discuss the relationship between Galatians 5 and Colossians 2.

∾ What is the answer to self-made religion and man-made rules?

## THOUGHT FOR THE WEEK

If we believe a lie, we submit ourselves to the decrees of a legalistic religion that seeks to control us through a list of rules and regulations. I know this is not how you want to live. No one wants to live in bondage when they can live in freedom.

While all lies will place us in bondage, Paul has a specific lie in mind. The lie is that Jesus Christ is not enough. The lie says that we need Jesus plus rules or works or . . . But the truth is that in Him we are complete. There is nothing to add. We have been given the righteousness of Christ, and it is enough. Rest in that freedom. Relax in Him.

All religions other than Christianity are focused on man striving to find, or even to be, God—Christianity alone is God finding man. All other religions are man trying to build a road to the top of the mountain to find God. There is a road, only one, but it did not start at the bottom. It started at the top, when Christ came down to earth. All other religions teach that man can work to be better. Christianity makes man new so he *is* better. We have seen the truth of who Christ is; now we are seeing who we are in Christ. He is everything we need.

# THAT *I* MAY WALK
# IN A *MANNER* WORTHY

What's the difference between being in bondage to a set of rules and behaving as a believer? Have you struggled to find the balance you need to walk the way you should? What is the truth about living the Christian life? This week's study will help you better understand the truth.

## DAY ONE

Read Colossians 3 and mark every reference to *Jesus Christ.* Include the word *Lord* if it refers to Christ. If you believe a reference is to God the Father, don't mark it. List in your notebook what you learn.

The emphasis in Colossians 1 is on who Christ is and what He has done. In chapter 2, the emphasis is on who we are in Him. What is the emphasis in Colossians 3 concerning Christ and our relationship to Him? Don't forget to record your insights in your notebook.

Paul begins describing Christ in chapter 1 and sums up his description in chapter 3. From your list about Christ, choose one description that sums up everything Paul has said about our Lord and Savior. (Keep in mind the word *all* is used frequently in describing Christ.)

## DAY TWO

In chapter 3 Paul moves from who Christ is and what we have in Him, to how we are to live. To live free from bondage to self-made religion and rules with victory over the flesh, we must understand that we are complete in Christ. There is nothing to add. We have everything we need to live as who we are: a child of God.

Read Colossians 3:1-11, paying close attention to the phrases "old self" and "new self." Watch for the contrast Paul is making.

If your Bible has marginal notes, take a moment to see if it gives you an alternate translation for "self." If so, you will see that "man" is another way of translating the Greek word for "self."

Sometimes it is helpful to see how a phrase is used elsewhere in the Bible. Read Romans 6:1-11 and Ephesians 4:17-24 to familiarize yourself with this phrase.

## DAY THREE

You learned yesterday that our "old man" was crucified with Christ. He is dead and we have put on a new man. In other words, we have been born again. If the old man is dead, then it makes sense that we should not behave the way the old man did.

Start a comparison chart which will show you the characteristics of the old man and the new man. In your notebook, draw a two-column chart like the one illustrated on the next page. Read Colossians 3:5-11. List under "Old Man" all the things we're to consider ourselves dead to or are to put aside.

| Old Man | New Man |
|---------|---------|
|         |         |

## DAY FOUR

Today read Colossians 3:10-17 and add to your chart all the things that characterize the new man. When you have finished it, read over the chart. It is an overwhelming list, isn't it! How is it possible to live like this? What happened in Colossians 3:9,10? The old was put off and the new was put on.

## DAY FIVE

We saw yesterday an impressive list of behaviors that characterize the believer. As the elect of God, the chosen of God, the holy and beloved, we are a new creation. This list characterizes the behavior patterns of the new man.

Today read Galatians 5:19-23 and see if there is any comparison with what you have already seen. List in your notebook on the OLD MAN/NEW MAN chart the characteristics of the flesh under the OLD MAN. List the fruit of the Spirit under the NEW MAN.

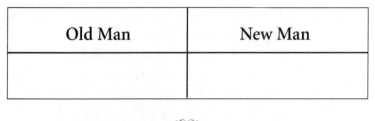

## DAY SIX

How do I walk in the reality of the new man? What is the difference between being under legalistic restrictions, as we were warned against in chapter 2, and walking the way Paul describes the new man?

Read Colossians 3:10 carefully and consider the word "knowledge." Cross-reference this passage with Colossians 1:9 and 2:2,3. Paul is restating what he said in verses 1 and 2 of this chapter. We must constantly be seeking the things above, always setting our mind on them. In other words, to walk consistently in obedience to the Spirit, we must consistently be studying the Word of God because it is what sets our focus on Christ. It is as simple as drawing near to Christ and focusing on Him.

## DAY SEVEN

Store in your heart: Colossians 3:12.

Read and discuss: Colossians 3; Romans 6:1-11; Galatians 5; Ephesians 4:17-24.

### QUESTIONS FOR DISCUSSION OR INDIVIDUAL STUDY

ᖷ What did you learn from chapter 3 this week about Jesus Christ? What exactly has Jesus done for us? How would you sum up what you've learned about Christ from your study of Colossians? Discuss the implications of what you've learned.

ᖷ Discuss or think about how it is possible to live the Christian life. What happened to the "old man"?

ᖷ You cross-referenced "old man" and "new man" in Romans 6:1-11 and Ephesians 4:17-24. Discuss what the Holy Spirit taught you as you charted the characteristics of each one.

∾ What did you learn as you cross-referenced Galatians 5? What does the flesh look like? What does the Spirit look like? What is the command or admonition in this passage? What will the fruit of obedience be? How will it be recognized?

∾ What does it mean to consider yourself dead to the things of this world? How is it possible?

∾ As you saw these truths this week, how did the Holy Spirit minister to you? Has your behavior or beliefs changed as a result of what God has shown you? If so, how?

## THOUGHT FOR THE WEEK

Jesus is all and in all. What else do you need? Whatever is required, you can do. Whatever you need, you have because Jesus is all and in all. You don't have to work hard to get God to accept you. If you are a true child of God, a new man or a new woman, then you are complete in Christ. God loves you and He is not angry with you. You are in Christ and He is in you.

The "New Man" list of proper behavior you made this week is not unreasonable. On the contrary, it is reasonable, even normal. When you gave your life to Christ, when you became a Christian, God linked you with Christ so that, in essence, you have been crucified with Him. The old man was crucified, cast aside, put off. The new man, who is being renewed to a true knowledge according to the image of the One who created him, was put on. Keep seeking the things above, and day by day you will become more and more like Christ.

In Colossians 3:5 we are commanded to "consider the members of your earthly body as dead to…." How do you consider yourself dead to these deeds of the flesh? You do it by an act of your will. You say no to sin. You lay aside the "old man." By an act of your will, you keep your mind set on things above. You have put on the "new man" who is constantly being renewed to a true knowledge according to the image of his Creator. This renewal is a process which is energized by constant exposure to the Word of God. As you stay in the Word and keep seeking the things above, you will look more and more like who you are in Christ, and less and less like who you were.

# THAT I MAY BE LIKE HIM

Now we know the truth about Jesus Christ and who we are in Him. But how does that work at home? How are you to relate to other family members? How are you to relate in the workplace? This week we will apply the truth of the new man you have put on.

## DAY ONE

Family relationships. Work relationships. This is where everyone sees if we are what we say we are.

Today read Colossians 3:18–4:1. In your notebook, make a chart similar to the one you made last week. This one needs five columns. Title the columns "Wives," "Husbands/ Fathers," "Children," "Slaves," and "Masters."

| Wives | Husbands/ Fathers | Children | Slaves | Masters |
|-------|-------------------|----------|--------|---------|
|       |                   |          |        |         |

You will fill in this chart over the next few days. Today list the instructions Paul gives for family relationships. List instructions to fathers under the heading "Husbands/ Fathers." Ask the Father to reveal your heart and actions regarding these instructions, and give Him permission to work a change in your life.

## DAY TWO

God has a heart for proper family relationships. As we saw yesterday, Paul wants us to understand God's heart in respect to these relationships. Today look at Ephesians 5:22–6:4, a parallel passage, to see what else you can learn about how to live within a family structure. Then on the chart you started yesterday in your notebook, list the instructions Paul gives here. Again, ask God to show you, as you study, if there is an area in which you need improvement since these instructions are given for you to follow.

## DAY THREE

How do we handle relationships outside of our immediate family? Read Colossians 3:22–4:1 and Ephesians 6:5-9. List Paul's instructions for slaves and masters. Of course, in our society we do not have slavery, but the principles apply well to employee/employer relationships. How are we to respond to those we work for and to those who work for us? Compare what we see here with Titus 2:9-14.

## DAY FOUR

Paul closes the practical part of this letter with some general instructions. Read Colossians 4:2-6 and list in your notebook the instructions he gives.

Also note Paul's personal prayer request. You began a list on prayer when we studied chapter 1. Add to it today. We saw what Paul prayed for those at Colossae and now we see what Paul desired to have them pray for him.

What would a typical prayer meeting look like if the major requests were for an open door to share the gospel? We pray for our health, wealth, and happiness. Paul wanted an open door to share the gospel. What a difference in focus!

## DAY FIVE

If the entire church of Jesus Christ were to follow the admonitions in Colossians 4:5,6, we would find more opportunity to share the gospel than we ever thought possible. When it comes to dealing with people outside the church, we are sometimes our own worst enemies. Read Colossians 4:5,6 and compare what you learn there with Ephesians 5:15,16.

Also read Colossians 4:7-18 and notice how important people are to Paul. People are more important than anything else, except our relationship to God. People are so important to Jesus that He died for us. Are individuals important to you? They should be. Invest some time in someone God has placed in your life.

## DAY SIX

As this study comes to a close, reflect on everything you have learned these last eight weeks. Today read over the list of what you have learned about Jesus Christ in the book of Colossians. Then take some time to meditate on what you have learned from Paul's instructions.

Spend the rest of your time in prayer, thanking God for such an awesome Savior and making a commitment to keep setting your mind on things above, and not on the things of earth.

## DAY SEVEN

Store in your heart: Colossians 4:5,6.
Read and discuss: Colossians 3:12–4:18.

*QUESTIONS FOR DISCUSSION OR INDIVIDUAL STUDY*

∾ What are the instructions for the men of the family in Colossians? In Ephesians? How can a man love his wife and not be embittered against her? What are some practical ways? How can a man discipline his children and not exasperate them?

∾ How are wives to live in the family in light of what you have seen this week in Colossians? In Ephesians?

∾ What is the responsibility of children within the family structure? Who would be responsible to teach them these responsibilities? If you're a parent, share how you do this. You can learn from one another.

∾ What did the Holy Spirit teach you as you studied these instructions to the family?

∾ What is our response to be to those outside the family?

∾ As employees, how are we to respond to our employers? What is the difference between external service and sincerity of heart? How should I respond to a contrary, difficult boss? For whom am I really working? How then, am I to work?

ം As an employer, how am I to treat those who work for me? Why?

ം Discuss practical ways to behave with wisdom toward the lost.

ം Many people say religion is a personal issue only. It is between me and God alone. Is our Christianity to be personal only, or is there to be an effect on those around us? How should my relationship with Jesus Christ affect those around me?

ം What was Paul's prayer request? How should this affect my prayer requests? Have you prayed in this manner this week? What has the Holy Spirit shown you?

## THOUGHT FOR THE WEEK

Is everything that you do a reflection of the name of Jesus? In Colossians 3:17 Paul writes, "Whatever you do in word or deed, do all in the name of the Lord Jesus". Are your actions reflecting who you are? What impressions do your actions give about the kingdom of God?

When speaking about relationships, Paul's first command is to wives. Wives are to be subject to their husbands. Three things about this verse are very important, but sometimes overlooked. First, the verb tense in Greek indicates that the action by the wife is voluntary. In other words, she is not forced to obey by a demanding, overbearing husband. She chooses to be submissive because of her personal relationship to Jesus Christ. Second, her action is motivated by a husband who loves his wife as stated in verse 19. The third thing is that this action is "fitting in the Lord" or proper in the scheme of Christianity.

In the culture to which Paul is writing, this attitude actually elevated women beyond societal norms. In most cultures, the obedience of the wife was not an issue because the wife had no real rights and therefore no alternative. Paul gave the woman responsibility to decide what she would do because, in the Lord, male and female are equal. The issue is an issue of authority, not equality. Every institution must have a head, and the home is no exception. Wives, pray through this study and seek God's face. I know that for some this sounds like a difficult teaching, but if you choose obedience to God, He provides grace to do what He has called you to do. Husbands, the issue of being under the authority of the husband is between your wife and God.

Paul demanded of the husband that he treat his wife with a self-sacrificing love, not a self-satisfying love. The husband is not to be embittered against his wife. The word "embittered" could also be translated "harsh." Husbands, are you harsh with your wife? Do you treat her gently, as a delicate flower to be cared for? Is your tone of voice usually sharp or biting when she interrupts what you are doing or what you are watching? Is your love for her self-sacrificing? Would you sacrifice sports or a hobby or some other interest to spend time with her?

Fathers, which probably should include both parents, are commanded not to exasperate their children. The idea is to not discipline them in such a way that your children lose heart. Proper discipline is an essential and missing element in parenting today. But when we need to discipline our children we should remember that it was not designed by God to break their spirits!

Paul cared for people. God loves people. Jesus died for people. We are to handle people gently, because we are dealing with someone God values highly. Do you see people as individually important? Jesus summed up the commandments into just two. You remember them, don't you? You shall love the Lord your God. . . . You shall love your neighbor as yourself.

This has been our goal in this study. First, that you would know God better and therefore love Him more. And second, by being obedient to what the Holy Spirit has taught you, that you would love your neighbor as yourself. This has been a great study. May God bless you, and give you a hunger for His Word. May you walk in a manner worthy of the Lord.

# COLOSSIANS AT A GLANCE

**Theme of Colossians:**

| | CHAPTER THEMES | *Author:* |
|---|---|---|
| | 1 | |
| | | *Historical Setting:* |
| | 2 | *Purpose:* |
| | | *Key Words:* |
| | 3 | |
| | 4 | |

# NOTES

## PHILIPPIANS

1. NIV: *brothers*

2. NIV: also *glad, boast*

   KJV: also *gladness*

   NKJV: also *glad, gladness*

3. The NIV uses *mind* only one time. In 1:27, it translates *mind* as "as one man" and in 2:3 it translates *humility of mind* as *humility*. It also uses *think(s)* and *like-minded*. Therefore, if you are using the NIV, watch carefully for these "substitutes." This is one of the reasons we recommend the NAS.

   NKJV: also *like-minded, thinks, meditate*

   KJV: also *likeminded, think*

4. NIV: also *think*

   NKJV: *think*

   KJV: *minded*

5. NIV; NKJV: *chains*

   KJV: *bonds*

6. NIV: also *petition*

7. NIV: also *something, whatever, everything*

8. NIV: also *situation*

   KJV; NKJV: *state; in all things*

9. NIV: also *glad, boast*

   KJV: also *gladness*

   NKJV: also *glad, gladness*

10. NIV: *mind, humility, man, think(s)*, and *like-minded*

    NKJV: also *like-minded, thinks,* and *meditate*

    KJV: also *likeminded* and *think*

## COLOSSIANS

1. KJV; NKJV: *word of the truth*
2. NIV: also *know*
   KJV: also *acknowledgment*
3. NIV: also *wise*
4. NIV: also *every (way), everything, full*
   KJV: also *every*
   NKJV: also *fully, every*

# Notes for Personal Study

# Notes for Personal Study

# NOTES FOR PERSONAL STUDY

# Notes for Personal Study

# Notes for Personal Study

# NOTES FOR PERSONAL STUDY

# NOTES FOR PERSONAL STUDY

# Notes for Personal Study

# BOOKS IN THE
# NEW INDUCTIVE STUDY SERIES

જ્જ્જ્જ્

*Teach Me Your Ways*
Genesis, Exodus,
Leviticus, Numbers,
Deuteronomy

*Choosing Victory,
Overcoming Defeat*
Joshua, Judges, Ruth

*Desiring God's Own Heart*
1 & 2 Samuel,
1 Chronicles

*Come Walk in My Ways*
1 & 2 Kings, 2 Chronicles

*Overcoming Fear and
Discouragement*
Ezra, Nehemiah, Esther

*God's Blueprint for
Bible Prophecy*
Daniel

*The Call to Follow Jesus*
Luke

*The Holy Spirit
Unleashed in You*
Acts

*God's Answers for
Relationships and Passions*
1 & 2 Corinthians

*Free from Bondage
God's Way*
Galatians, Ephesians

*That I May Know Him*
Philippians, Colossians

*Standing Firm in
These Last Days*
1 & 2 Thessalonians

*Walking in Power, Love,
and Discipline*
1 & 2 Timothy, Titus

*Living with Discernment
in the End Times*
1 & 2 Peter, Jude

*Behold, Jesus Is Coming!*
Revelation

# HARVEST HOUSE BOOKS
## BY KAY ARTHUR

❧❧❧❧

Beloved
God, Are You There?
How to Study Your Bible
Israel, My Beloved (A Novel)
Lord, Teach Me to Pray in 28 Days
A Marriage Without Regrets
A Marriage Without Regrets Study Guide
A Moment with God
My Savior, My Friend
Speak to My Heart, God
With an Everlasting Love (A Novel)

### *Discover 4 Yourself*
### *Inductive Bible Studies for Kids*

How to Study Your Bible for Kids
God's Amazing Creation (Genesis 1–2)
Digging Up the Past (Genesis 3–11)
Joseph—God's Superhero (Genesis 37–50)
Wrong Way, Jonah! (Jonah)
Jesus in the Spotlight (John 1–11)
Jesus—Awesome Power, Awesome Love (John 11–16)
Jesus—To Eternity and Beyond! (John 17–21)
Boy, Have I Got Problems! (James)
Lord, Teach Me to Pray for Kids

## *...Everybody, Everywhere, Anytime, Anyplace, Any Age...*
### Can Discover the Truth for Themselves

In today's world with its often confusing and mixed messages, where can you turn to find the answer to the challenges you and your family face? Whose word can you trust? Where can you turn when you need answers—about relationships, your children, your future?

## The <u>Updated</u> New Inductive Study Bible

Open *this* study Bible and you will soon discover its uniqueness—unlike any other, this study Bible offers no notes, commentaries, or the opinions of others telling you what the Scripture is saying. It is in fact the only study Bible based entirely on the *inductive* study approach, providing you with instructions and the tools for observing what the text really says, interpreting what it means, and applying its principles to your life.

The only study Bible containing the *inductive study method* taught and endorsed by Kay Arthur and Precept Ministries.

• A new *smaller* size makes it easier to carry • individualized instructions for studying *every* book • guides for color marking keywords and themes • *Updated* NASB text • *improved* in-text maps and charts • 24 pages of full-color charts, historical timelines, & maps • self-discovery in its truest form

*The Message, The Bible.*
*The Method, Inductive.*

A SIMPLE, PROVEN APPROACH TO LETTING GOD'S WORD CHANGE YOUR LIFE...FOREVER

## HARVEST HOUSE™
### PUBLISHERS
EUGENE, OREGON

# DIGGING DEEPER

Books in the New Inductive Study Series are survey courses. If you want to do a more in-depth study of a particular book of the Bible, we suggest that you do a Precept Upon Precept Bible Study Course on that book. The Precept studies require approximately five hours of personal study a week. You may obtain more information on these powerful courses by contacting Precept Ministries International at 800-763-8280, visiting our website at www.precept.org, or filling out and mailing the response card in the back of this book.

If you desire to expand and sharpen your skills, you would really benefit by attending a Precept Ministries Institute of Training. The Institutes are conducted throughout the United States, Canada, and in a number of other countries. Class lengths vary from one to five days, depending on the course you are interested in. For more information on the Precept Ministries Institute of Training, call Precept Ministries.